Wandering Reminiscence

OrangeBooks Publication

Smriti Nagar, Bhilai, Chhattisgarh - 490020

Website: **www.orangebooks.in**

First Edition, 2023

WANDERING REMINISCENCE

A DESIRE TO BE HEARD

AAMINA SADIYA ALI

OrangeBooks Publication
www.orangebooks.in

Preface

Dear Reader,

As I sit down to write this preface, I am filled with a sense of excitement and nervousness. At just 16 years old, I am still figuring out who I am and who I want to be, but one thing that has always been a constant in my life is my passion for poetry and literature.

Ever since I was young, I have found solace in the written word. Whether it was losing myself in the pages of a novel or analyzing the works of renowned poets, literature has always been my escape. But as I grew older, I began to develop my own voice and perspective, and I found myself drawn to the art form of poetry. Writing poetry has become a way for me to express myself and make sense of the world around me. Through my words, I hope to connect with others who may feel the same way, to help them feel seen and heard.

The purpose of writing this book is not only to share my words with the world, but also to understand if people agree with the way I think and to learn from the experience. It's a way for me to check my vibe, so to speak, and to spread awareness on some topics that I feel are important. I hope that by reading my poems, you too can feel a sense of connection and understanding.

Each poem in this book is a reflection of my personal experiences, the ups and downs that have shaped me into the person I am today. They are a part of me, and I hope that in sharing them, I can help others feel more comfortable being themselves.

Writing this book has been a journey, one that has allowed me to explore my thoughts and feelings in a way that I never have before. And as I take this next step in my journey, I am grateful for the opportunity to share my words with you.

Sincerely,

Aamina Sadiya Ali.

Acknowledgement

Dear, everyone who I want to thank,

I want to take a moment to express my deepest gratitude to each and every one of you. Your presence in my life has made me the poet I am today, and I could not have done it without you.

Dear, mamma you were the one who first introduced me to the beauty of language and taught me how to rhyme. You have always been my biggest cheerleader, and your unwavering support has given me the confidence to pursue my passion. I will never forget the countless hours we spent together, crafting verses and exploring new forms of expression. Your influence on my life and my writing cannot be overstated.

Dear, papa, I know that you have always wanted the best for me, and I hope that my success as a poet will make you proud. Your belief in me has always been a source of strength, and I am grateful for your unwavering support.

Dear, Yumna, you are my dear little sister, but you are also so much more than that. You have been my first reader since I started writing, and your feedback has helped me grow as a writer. Your honesty and support have been invaluable, and I am grateful for your presence in my life (even if I wanted a brother all along).

Dear, Disha, you have been my best friend for over a decade, and I cannot imagine this journey without you. You have been with me through every poem I've ever written, and your unwavering support has been a constant source of strength. Thank you for always believing in me and for encouraging me to keep going, even when things got tough.

Dear, Veda, even if I wanted to write a book my entire life, you are the reason I started and finished it. It was your creative energy and encouragement that sparked me and I am forever grateful for that. Your support and guidance have helped me through some of my toughest writing challenges, and I am excited to see what we can create together in the future.

To all of my friends who have supported me along the way, thank you. You have been my cheerleaders and my sounding boards, and I am grateful for each and every one of you. Each heartbreak and friendship poem you made me write ,peaked a different folder in me.Your well wishes and encouragement have given me the confidence to keep going, even when things got tough.

To my extended family, who do not even know I write poetry. I want to thank you for your opinions and support. I know that this part of me may be new to you, but your perspectives and insights are valuable to me. Thank you for being a part of my journey and for supporting me in ways both big and small.

To my seventh-grade English teacher who gave me the chance to explore poetry, thank you. Without your support and encouragement, I may have never discovered this passion of mine. And to all of the other teachers who may have doubted the practicality of studying literature, I hope to prove you wrong. Poetry can be profitable, and I will continue to work hard to show that to the world.

To my childhood best friends for whom every word of poetry was written, I want to thank you for existing. You have been my muse and my inspiration, and your presence in my life has given my writing a depth and intensity that I never knew was possible. Thank you for being a part of my journey and for inspiring me to create some of my strongest work.

To my readers, I cannot express my gratitude enough. Your support and feedback have been integral to my growth as a writer, and I am honored to have you as a part of my audience. Whether you have been with me from the beginning or just discovering my work now, thank you for taking the time to explore my words.

To my enemies, I want to thank you too. Your actions may have hurt me in the moment, but they have also inspired some of my most powerful work.

To the auto-correct that has saved me from my terrible spelling, and to the dictionary and electronic devices that have aided my writing, thank you for existing and making my craft possible.

My emotions have also played a significant role in my poetry. To the ones that have swirled and created strong winds within me, pushing me to express myself in new and creative ways, I thank you for your powerful influence.

Lastly, to myself, I am overflowing with pride for how far I have come on this journey. I have reached a new step, and I am excited to continue exploring the path ahead, to see where my words will take me next.

Sincerely,

Aamina .

Book Summary

In this poetry collection, the author explores a wide range of emotions and experiences. In "The Fractured Realm," the author delves into the depths of sadness, brokenness, and tears. Through these poems, the reader is invited to witness the author's raw and vulnerable moments, as she navigates the complexities of life and relationships.

In "The Void," the author explores the feelings of youth and the sense of void that often accompanies it. She delves into the idea of escaping into other worlds and using imagination as a coping mechanism. Through these poems, the author captures the essence of the struggle that many young people face as they try to find their place in the world.

In "Beyond the Surface," the author delves into a variety of human experiences, from love and loss to hope and despair. She invites the reader to look beyond the surface of these experiences and to explore the deeper emotions and meanings that lie beneath.

Finally, in "States of Mind," the author tackles the important topic of mental health and well-being. Through her poems, she explores the complexities of the human mind, and the emotions that come with it. She encourages the reader to be kind and compassionate to themselves, and to seek help when needed.

Overall, this poetry collection is a journey through the many facets of the human experience. Through her words, the author invites the reader to connect with her on a personal level, and to explore the depths of their own emotions and experiences.

Index

The Fractured Realm

The Void

The Fractured Realm

Hope?

Why do we cling on to that last bit of hope?

When everything else seems to be falling apart,

When the world feels like a dark and empty slope,

And the future looks bleak and devoid of heart,

Why do we hold on to that final shred,

Of faith in something that may never come,

When logic and reason fill us with dread,

And our dreams seem distant and overrun?

Perhaps it is the human need to believe,

That there is still a chance for things to be right,

That the universe has a trick up its sleeve,

And will turn our fortunes with a sudden light,

Or maybe it's just the fear of letting go,

Of admitting defeat and giving in,

Of facing the truth that we may never know,

What could have been if we had just believed again,

Whatever the reason, we hold on tight,

To that last bit of hope that keeps us sane,

Through the darkest of days and the longest of nights,

And gives us the strength to try once again,

So let us cling to hope with all our might,

And never give up on what we truly believe,

For in that final glimmer of light,

Lies the power to achieve what we perceive,

Why do we cling on to that last bit of hope?

As if it's a lifeline, a rope to hold,

In the darkest moments, when we feel alone,

Hope is the light, that guides us home,

It's the glimmer in the distance, that we can't ignore,

The promise of a better tomorrow, that were fighting for,

It's the belief that things can change, that keeps us going,

Even when the winds of adversity, are fiercely blowing,

Hope is the force, that pushes us to try,

To rise up from the ashes, and reach for the sky,

It's the fuel for our dreams, the spark in our eyes,

The reason why we don't give up, even when we're tired.

Gone

I still can't face the fact you went away,
You did'nt let me convince you to stay,
There hasn't been a single that
I havent thought about you,
After all you were responsible for all that I do,
So you had to see me grow up,
When i get married help me with my make up.

I do get sad and I do shed a tear,
When you were here everything was crystal clear,
Everyday things remind me of you,
When i look at it , i feel sorrow and pleasure too,
I wish you could magically appear,
You gave me a million memories to treasure.

We were yet to have fun,
You were so different from everyone.
You were supposed to see how I make you proud,
Do you still watch me from above the cloud?

Even though now we are far apart,
I can still feel you close to my heart.
You were always my hero,
You made me laugh, so I give you a million, not zero.

But you dont have to be sad , cause it's okay,

We're managing anyway,

I hope you're looking at me now,

Is the promise of heaven, wow.

However, I know you're there with me,

But I still regret that I can't see.

Just Sad

Sadness lurks within my heart,

A constant presence, never to depart.

It weighs me down, tearing me apart,

Leaving me empty, a shell of my former self,
a work of art.

Tears fall like rain, a never-ending shower,

As I try to make sense of this endless power

That sadness holds over me, hour by hour,

Leaving me broken, a wilted flower.

I long for the light, for a glimmer of hope,

But it seems so far away, like a beam through a telescope.

I try to hold on, try to find a way to cope,

But it's hard when sadness feels like a heavy yoke.

I know I must keep going, keep fighting the fight,

But sometimes it feels like I'm lost in the night,

Like there's no way out, no end in sight,

Just darkness and sadness, an endless plight.

Feel Me

I am afraid to be owned,

Like a massacre due to possession,

They say someone will understand,

Someone will get you,

Just as much as you do,

Spiraling through the lost connection,

maybe your hate will continue,

But choices remain undetermined,

When white will darken black,

When the winds of east travel north,

When the fantasy consumes reality,

When lost will be found,

And when truth will lie,

But the soul will break through,

It will corrupt the safer you try to keep it,

So start teaching defense,

Don't hide the world with your shadow,

Try to seek it within,

Answer: why are there hues over her skin?

And some things should be kept in the safe ,

Unspoken and counted as devious ,

when you can't understand what it means,

Are you not but an illiterate,

 who chooses to see those eyes glisten,

But yet decides to tear it up,

When the whole outfit is decided by its shoes,

Ever thought how unfair the concept seems?

Hear me this one time ,

And let loose your guard,

Let them not be caught up in the kite string,

Get to know what world they wish ,

Free the burdened,

Calm yourself and stay relieved,

Because denial always comes before acceptance.

Soar

I am anonymous, a soul unknown,

With a heart that bleeds and a mind that's blown,

The agony I feel is raw and intense,

As my brain blues and my nerves feel the offense,

The claws of pain grip me tight,

As I try to break free with all my might,

The wavy emotions that rage within,

Are like a storm that I cannot win,

The tune claims to die, as the fields turn cold,

And the white death steals the stories untold,

The drinks that once soothed my soul,

Now bring me closer to my ultimate goal,

The touch of hope that once brought healing,

Now feels like a trap that I'm slowly sealing,

The hole in my heart that nothing fits,

Is a reminder of all that I've missed,

The impossible hours that bring fame,

Are the ones that leave me feeling the shame,

The distant fire that rebels the chains,

Is a reminder of all that I could gain,

Flash of memories, of my past behavior,

Remind me of the young and foolish traitor,

But I won't let that define my fate,

For I know that I am stronger than hate,

The Hale consumes me, but I won't let go,

For I am a fighter, a warrior, and I know,

That even though the battle is tough,

I don't lose, for I am enough,

So I'll rise from the ashes, like gold,

And let my story be forever told,

For I am anonymous no more,

And I won't lose this battle, I will soar.

When I Shatter

Crashing the ink ,

The paper drips sapphire,

Yields the crap never listed,

Liquidation of raw declaration,

The accusations of unseen flaws,

Facing an alliance with the dicey,

Meddling with impotence and power alike,

Bound , held up yet concealed,

The symphony stops as the air sets in,

When the district fluid flows the same direction,

Eyes splashing emerald,

And what can be seen prevents the diction,

The proclaim will be shed,

And bluff will continue to reign,

Barriers lengthen towards the sky,

And the episode culminates.

Coping

Confusion fills my mind each day ,
As I struggle to find my way ,
The choices I must make I fear ,
Are leading me to what I hold dear,

Am I becoming what I've always hated?
Falling into the life I once berated
Death looms ahead, I can see it clear
But I'm lost, and I don't know what to do here,

I thought I knew my path to take ,
But now, my heart begins to ache ,
The fear of failure, the fear of pain ,
It's hard to stay positive when I feel the strain,

I don't want to live in fear and doubt ,
I want to rise above, I want to shout ,
That I can be strong, and I can be true ,
And find my way, in all that I do,

So I'll keep searching, for what's right ,

And keep hoping, I'll find the light ,

And though the journey may be rough ,

I'll keep moving forward, I've had enough.

Whispers From Beyond

My friend, my confidant, a shining star,
18 years old, yet so bright, so far
But the world can be cruel, and harsh words fly
Society's pressure, too much for her to try

I remember the day, when you slipped away
Taken by the pain, no more words to say
I was lost, my heart in shambles and debris
Wondering why the world couldn't just let you be

But as the days passed, and tears fell like rain
I realized, your passing was not in vain
For through the hardship and the endless grief
I learned some valuable lessons, some relief

I learned that life is fragile, and should be cherished
That every soul is special, and should never be perished
I learned that love and kindness are the way
And to always stand up against hate and dismay

I learned that you will always live on

In the memories, that will forever stay strong

In the laughter, and the moments we shared

In the love, that was never to be impaired

So my dear friend, as I lay this poem at your feet

I hope that you know, your life was meaningful and
sweet

And though you may be gone, your legacy lives on

In the hearts of those who loved you, and in the things
that you've done

Hardships I faced, were immense, unbearable at times

the weight of your loss, felt like a crime

But with each passing day, the weight lightens

and the sun shines brighter, the hope tightens

You, my dear friend, who left us too soon

In your passing, you've inspired us to be kind, to be true

You were the light in the darkness, the hope in the gloom

I will always love you, not a shadow, not a boon.

Silent Plea

In the cold and lonely nights
I stare up at the starry sights
My heart is heavy, my soul is tired
And I am so very, very uninspired

My dreams are shattered, my hopes are gone
The weight of the world feels like a ton
I'm tired of feeling abandoned and alone
And all my tears feel like stone

I know my time here is nearly through
And my last words are meant for you
Please don't give up, please don't despair
Find hope in the love that others share

My journey may be ending, but yours has just begun
Believe in yourself and all that can be done
Life is a gift, a precious treasure
So hold on tight to every measure

Goodbye dear world, it's time for me to part

Know that you will always be in my heart

Remember my words, my final plea

Love each other and always be free.

This Is What Failure Feels Like

Perhaps I should embrace the flames,
And face the academy's brutal games.
But my desires and loves will not fade,
And my blood will not be their trade.

The chains may tangle, and my breath choke,
But my soul will not be broken or broke.
My tears may flow, but I'll not be fed
To hungry dogs, as they crave for the dead.

My bones will not be crushed or shattered,
Nor my body torn and battered.
And though dying may feel like release,
My spirit will never rest in peace.

This failure feels like my own claws,
Tearing at my skin with its cruel jaws.
I'm suffocating, and my chest feels tight,
How can I ease this pain and find the light?

Perhaps I'll let the darkness lead me raw,

But I know that's not what I'm looking for.

Do I choose what others call evil and vile,

And test my limits to the extreme mile?

But to do that, I must kill my dreams,

And drown in hurt's endless streams.

Is it worth it to block out the sound,

And let my fears drag me to the ground?

Pathetic

I stand amidst the ruins of my dreams,

The remnants of my efforts, torn apart at the seams.

The weight of failure heavy on my chest,

As I struggle to find a way to rest.

I gave my all, poured my heart and soul,

Into the pursuit of success, of achieving my goal.

But despite my best efforts, it all fell apart,

Leaving me stranded, broken, and scarred.

The voices of doubt, of self-criticism,

Echo in my mind, with unrelenting rhythm.

I feel like a failure, a disappointment to all,

And wonder if I'm even worth the effort at all.

The fear of the unknown, the uncertainty ahead,

Paralyze me, leaving me lost and unfed.

How do I move forward, when all I feel is pain,

When my hopes and dreams have gone down the drain?

Frozen Flames

Numb reflections, forgotten memories

Lay dormant in the depths of our souls

We stay silent, afraid to awaken

The frozen flames that still burn

We let them rise, higher and higher

Until the heat consumes us whole

The pain, the hurt, the anger and fear

All fuelling the flames that won't let go

We hold tight to the numbness within

Afraid of what we'll find if we let it out

The memories we've tried to forget

Still there, lurking in the shadows of doubt

But what if we faced them, head on

The numbness, the memories, the fear?

What if we let the frozen flames rise

And finally let them burn clear?

Maybe then we could break free

From the chains that bind us tight

Maybe then we could heal and grow

And find the strength to shine bright

So let the numbness fade away

And embrace the memories that remain

Speak out, let your voice be heard

And let the frozen flames burn away the pain.

Is It A Trap?

Cold whispers in my mind,

Telling me to embrace the fire of passion,

To welcome the drifts of sorrow,

And listen to the echoes that call my name.

Clutch my soul, they say,

As the feeling bangs my head,

My brain wants to explode,

My heart wants to stop racing.

My limbs feel petrified,

My eyes lack vision,

My nose lacks smell,

 My ears can't hear,

And my tongue can't taste.

My body can't feel,

But I still sense the danger.

Is this the path I should take?

Should I let go of all control?

Or should I hold on tight,

And fight against this tempting call?

The fire of passion burns bright,

But it can also consume,

The drifts of sorrow may offer solace,

But they can also suffocate.

The echoes may sound alluring,

But they can also deceive.

I must weigh the risks and rewards,

Of giving in to this temptation,

I must be strong and resolute,

And not let my judgment be clouded.

For the danger is real,

And the consequences could be dire,

I must listen to the cold whispers,

But I must also listen to my own voice.

In the end, I will make my choice,

And accept the consequences that follow,

 But I will do so with a clear mind,

And not let the whispers control me.

The Real Her

A constant foe within her mind,

The battle rages on, unkind,

Her confidence, fragile and weak,

The struggle to believe, a fight to seek,

An anchor of fear, holding her down,

Voices of the crowd, a deafening sound,

She's not a bad person, just shy,

Preferring solitude, away from prying eyes,

Interested in the idea of crime,

Writing her thoughts down in rhyme,

Addicted to coffee and books,

An independent spirit, she fiercely looks,

Living but wanting to die,

Misunderstood, people pass her by,

Assumptions of a serial killer,

Silence mistaken for something much iller,

Now she wants the world to see,

The real her, not who they perceive to be,

Whispers now replace the shouts of fame,

Breaking free from thoughts that bring shame,

Angry, so angry, her power scares,

Yet no one sees beyond her outer layers,

Regrets for those who disregard her presence,

A listener, finding solace in the stars luminescence.

Mortal Beauty

The sky is so tragically beautiful,

A graveyard of stars, lost and dutiful.

But amidst the darkness, a light still lives,

A reminder to stay alive and forgive.

Sorry I know my words can kill,

But I promise to try and be still.

I was getting better, but not again,

Falling back to where I've always been.

The masked girl, hidden in plain sight,

With dark aesthetic vibes that come to light.

A wolf within, fierce and strong,

But brittle yet angelic, where do I belong?

An overthinker, drowning in silence,

She turned her emotions off with such violence.

Sometimes we need to kill ourselves to stay alive,

To fight the demons and learn to thrive.

And when her halo broke, shattered in two,

She carved the halves into horns, a symbol anew.

Hazel eyes that hold both light and dark,

Beautiful in her imperfections, a work of art.

Trial

I worked so hard and gave it my all

But somehow, I still managed to fall

I failed my goal and now I feel small

Like a tiny speck, too small to recall

I feel awful, like I'm stuck in a rut

Like everything I do is just meaningless,
just a blip in time's cut

I feel dead inside, like my spirit's been shut

Like there's no hope, no light, no luck

I try to hold on, try to keep the faith

But it's hard when everything seems to be laced

With failure and disappointment, a never-ending race

Towards a goal that seems further away, at an
unreachable pace

I don't know how to break free from this prison

This cycle of sadness, this endless revision

Of my failures and mistakes, an endless decision

To keep going, or to give up and let go of my ambition

But I know I can't give up, not yet

I have to keep trying, I can't regret

The effort and hard work I've put

Into reaching my goal, I canTt let it be cut

So I'll keep fighting, keep pushing through

I wonTt let my failures define me, I'll start anew

I'll find a way to succeed, I'll make it true

I wonTt let my dreams die, I'll see them come true.

Sorry

Sorry, sorry, always sorry
Adding it at the end of my story
My words are my shield, my protection
Carefully chosen to avoid rejection

I fear my words will ruin it all
Days, months, years to recover from the fall
So I say sorry, just in case
Hoping it won't leave a permanent trace

Sorry for who I am in society's ropes
Tied and bound, with no room for hopes
I apologize even if it's not my fault
Words escaping me like a runaway colt

Sorry for stumbling and drawing life's steps
Trying my best to dodge all the missteps
Sorry for the way I am, for the way I act
Words cutting deep like a sharp, cold fact

Apologizing for asking questions, for not knowing
Wishing my mind was more sharp, more glowing
Sorry for being a waste of space, a burden
Feeling like I'm a mistake, something to be undone

Sorry for existing, for being here at all
Sorry for every stumble, every fall
I'm just sorry, and I wish it wasn't so
But it's the only way I know how to go.

Tattoo

Tear, a word with two sides to behold

Both tearing apart and tearing up, so bold

A symbol of strength, a reminder to endure

A tattoo on my wrist, to keep my past pure

My bark, like a tree, bears the marks of time

Cracks that signify, the struggles of the climb

But like the tree, I stay confident and strong

For I know the depths from where I belong

Tear, a force to reckon with, personified

Like a raging storm, that can't be denied

Yet also like a gentle breeze, that brings calm

Emotions that sweep over, like a healing balm

Knowing I was strong, a fact twisted and turned

As I drown in the bay, the lessons learned

But with Tear, a symbol of resilience and hope

I'll rise again, like a phoenix that can cope

This tattoo on my wrist, a constant reminder

Of the battles fought, and the victories kinder

A reflection of my heart, my soul, my mind

A testament to the past, yet staying aligned

With a future that's bright, and full of promise

Something i will always cherish

I wear this tattoo, like a badge of honor

I am powerful ,not a goner

For Tear, a word that means so much more

Is a symbol of my strength, that's at the core.

Not Made Of Glass

They say I'm delicate, a fragile flower,

But they don't know me, the depth of my power.

They call me glass, easily broken and shattered,

But I'll shred their hearts, for I am not a puppet to be flattered.

I don't want to be a girl, molded and shaped,

I want to run away, escape from the charade.

I want to be the villain, to break the mold,

To stop spreading light and embrace the cold.

Forced for my own good, but tired and done,

I don't want to pretend in a hive of bees, not one.

I need someone to get me, to understand my fears,

But all I can say is that I'm afraid and in tears.

I want to scream, to let the beast out,

But I don't want to hurt them, to cause them to doubt.

I want to give up, but I don't know what to do,

Lost in the storm, not knowing what's true.

I am a force to be reckoned with, a tempest in the night,

A burning flame, with the power to ignite.

My soul is a warrior, with scars to prove my fight,

I am strong, I am fierce, I am a force of might.

So don't drag me down, don't clip my wings,

Let me fly, let me be the queen of my own things.

For I am not delicate, not made of glass,

I am a fierce warrior, and nothing can surpass.

The Blame Game

Her story remains untold,

Her actions often condemned,

But have you ever wondered,

What pain her heart may have penned?

She's the villain in the tale,

With no reasons to defend,

But don't forget, she's human too,

With emotions that never bend.

She's been hurt and left alone,

By those who swore to care,

And now she's making them pay,

For the cost they chose to bear.

But society will never accept her,

As she stands against the norm,

They see her as a monster,

But her heart beats with a storm.

She's like a wounded bird,

Flying against the wind,

Trying to find her way back,

To a place where she can mend.

So don't be quick to judge,

Or to point fingers and blame,

For the villain in the story,

Is just a person in pain.

She may not be perfect,

But she's trying to survive,

In a world that doesn't understand her,

Where she's never given a fair try.

So next time you see her,

Try to see beyond her mask,

For the villain in the story,

Maybe someone you could help unmask.

The Void

Beauty In Mystery

The world runs on invisible things,

A tapestry of beauty and mystery,

The delicate petals of a flower,

Unfolding in a graceful dance,

The wind that whispers through the trees,

Filling the room with its quiet presence,

But sometimes, beauty hides in plain sight,

Camouflaged by the chaos of the world,

We stand together or we fall alone,

In the face of life's endless unknown,

Yet regularity can smother our unique spark,

Dimming the fire within our hearts,

We question what our future holds,

And wonder if our passions will survive,

Would we rather be dead to those who reject us,

Then live as someone we're not?

We struggle with the boldness of our dreams,

Wondering if we deserve to chase them,

Passion and wrath can consume us,

A blaze that threatens to engulf our souls,

But in the midst of it all, light seeps in,

A mystery that we may never understand,

There is no restart, only the option to quit,

But we cling to hope and fight to survive,

Sarcastic comments and vows of loyalty,

Errors we make and moments of control,

Sometimes we fall, numb and slain,

But we rise again, stronger for the journey.

Changes

Life is just a violent ride,

A stormy sea having waves that collide,

Changes come like lightning strikes,

Blinding flashes that leave us in spikes,

Like a caterpillar in a cocoon,

We transform and emerge brand new,

Unrecognisable from who we once were,

Yet still anchored to the past's lure,

The world is a battlefield, a war zone,

Where every step feels like a lone drone,

When life's a game of trial and error,

Its mistakes leave us scarred forever,

We walk a tightrope, trying to find balance,

Trembling, falling, with each new challenge,

Our minds a kaleidoscope of emotions,

A raging river of thoughts and commotions,

Friends come and go, like the seasons,

Leaving behind memories and reasons,

Sometimes a helping hand, sometimes a knife,

Life's lessons often come at a steep price,

We're a flock of birds, taking flight,

Trying to find our place in the light,

All our insecurities and fears,

Like weights on our wings, holding us near,

The world is a canvas, and we the art,

Trying to create our masterpiece, playing our part,

Of a bigger picture, a grand design,

A life well-lived, our ultimate shrine,

Life is a bittersweet melody,

A symphony of joy and melancholy,

But with each new note, we learn and grow,

And like a phoenix, we rise from the ashes below.

Why Him?

Why must we force boys to bear the weight

Of the world upon their shoulders, so great

A burden to carry, a mantle to wear

Demanding they provide, or fail and despair

Why can't they bask in the sun's warm rays

Lying back on a hammock, lazy and dazed

While their wives toil and sweat in the fields

Bringing home the harvest, it surely yields

Why does society demand that they strive

To conquer the world, and keep dreams alive

When all they really want is peace and calm

To hear their heart's beat, like a soothing balm

Why can't they cry and show their fears

Like the storm that rages, and then clears

Why must they always be strong and brave

And hide their emotions, deep in a cave

Why can't they be like a willow tree

Bending and swaying, with a gentle breeze

Instead, we want them to be an oak

Strong and unyielding, against life's cruel stroke

But who decided that this is the way

Boys must live, from birth to their dying day

Why can't we just let them be who they are

And celebrate their differences, near and far

Let us break these chains that bind

And open our eyes to a new world, kind

Where boys can be nurtured, and free to roam

And women can flourish, and build their own home.

We Think

We are masters of overthinking,

Fuelled by fear and doubt,

Our minds play out every scenario,

Every "what if" is given clout.

We suffer in our thoughts,

As if they were reality,

Spending tears on an unpredictable future,

One that may never come to be.

We grip onto our worries,

Like a vice that won't let go,

As if we can control the outcome,

But really, we just suffer in our own echo.

Our minds become a battleground,

As we fight against ourselves,

Our fears and doubts like weapons,

That harm us more than any external cells.

We create a storm of chaos,

In a world that's yet to unfold,

We torture ourselves with the possibilities,

And forget that life is meant to be bold.

We must learn to release our grip,

On the things we cannot control,

To live in the present moment,

And let the future unfold.

For in the end, the future is unpredictable,

And we can't control what will come to pass,

So let's not spend our tears on what could be,

And instead, live our lives with a little more sass.

Let's be brave in the face of uncertainty,

And embrace the unknown,

For it's in these moments of discomfort,

That we truly grow and are shown.

So let go of your worries and fears,

And live your life with zeal,

For the future is just a concept,

And the present is where the magic is real.

A Teenage Quest

As a teen, you're on a quest,

To discover yourself, be your best,

It's a journey that's fun and new,

And one that's approachable too.

Explore your passions, let them guide,

Be vivid, let your true self shine,

Engage in new experiences,

And open yourself to life's many instances.

Don't be afraid to try and fail,

For in those moments, you will prevail,

You'll learn and grow, and come to see,

The amazing person you can be.

So take a step, and then another,

And soon enough, you'll discover,

That the path to self-discovery,

Is one that's truly fulfilling and lovely.

A Teenage Quest -2

Teenagers face a world of change,

With challenges they must embrace.

Their bodies shift and hormones rage,

Their emotions run in every way.

Peer pressure is a constant force,

Pushing them to fit a mold.

They struggle to find their own voice,

In a world that's loud and bold.

School is a battleground of sorts,

With grades and tests and social scenes.

They strive to excel, but often fall short,

And feel the weight of other's dreams.

The future looms, a vast unknown,

With choices that must be made.

They search for purpose, for a place to call home,

But fear the paths that may lead astray.

Yet in this whirlwind of chaos and fear,

Teenagers hold a spark of hope.

A glimmer of light that's always near,

And gives them strength to learn and cope.

For they are brave, and they are strong,

With hearts that yearn to be free.

They'll face each challenge, right or wrong,

And carve a path that's uniquely their own, you'll see.

You Can

Rough times can make us feel so small,

But deep inside our hearts we know we can stand tall,

We must have faith in ourselves and our will,

To make it through this hard time we must have the skill.

We can't let our dreams be forgotten and fade,

No matter how hard our circumstances
may have weighed,

We must have the courage to go on and not break,

The light of hope will always be there to wake.

We can look to the stars to light our path,

And with faith and courage we can face the wrath,

Our strength will help us overcome any obstacle we face,

In this journey of life, we will find our place.

We must be patient and trust the process of time,

It will make us wiser, more loving and kind,

In the darkest of times, our courage will prevail,

Through strength and resilience, we will never fail.

We will learn to love ourselves and accept what's inside,

We will look forward to the future
and leave the past behind,

We will rise above all our doubts and fears,

And fill our lives with hope, love and good cheer.

We will fill our hearts with courage and strength,

And our lives will be filled with beauty and length,

We will take small steps and never give up,

Our dreams will come true and our lives will fill up.

We will never give in to fear,

We will be strong and hold evidence near,

We will have the courage to keep on going,

And make our dreams come alive with knowing.

Darkside

Deep within us lies a darker side

A shadowy realm where our demons reside

The side of us we try to hide away

The one we wish wouldn't see the light of day

The cruelty and hate that we can wield

The selfishness that makes our hearts unyield

The lies we tell and the harm we cause

The pain we inflict without a pause

We see it all around us, every day

The wars we wage, the innocent we slay

The greed that drives us to take and take

The corruption that leaves us in its wake

We try to justify it, make excuses

But the truth is there, and it seduces

The darkness in us that we can't deny

The part that makes us want to lie

But we must confront it, face the truth

Embrace the darkness in our youth

And learn to tame it, control the beast

So that our humanity can be at peace

For if we don't, the darkness will consume

And we'll be lost in its endless gloom

So let us face it, with courage and might

And shine a light on the darkness inside

Beneath the skin and bones we bear

Lie darker shades we hardly share

The shadowed corners of the mind

Where demons dwell and fears unwind

We strive to hide these parts away

To show the world a bright display

But deep within, we all have flaws

And secrets locked behind closed doors

While some delight in others pain

And revel in the hurt they gain

And still, there are those who deceive

And weave a web of lies to believe

They wear a mask to hide their face

And manipulate with practiced grace

These are the parts we seldom see

But they exist within you and me

The human race, a complex whole

With light and dark that make us whole

So let us not forget these sides

And seek to heal where darkness resides

For only when we face our fears

Can we move forward and dry our tears

Behold, the darkness that lies within

A side of us that's often seen as sin

A hunger for power, a thirst for control

These are the traits that can take a toll

Were capable of evil beyond belief

A twisted side that can cause us grief

We hurt and harm, we deceive and lie

All in the name of satisfying our pride

Were quick to judge and slow to forgive

We hold grudges, itTs hard to live

Were envious of others, we covet their wealth

Our greed knows no bounds, it's like a stealth

The dark side of humans is a scary place

It's where our fears and insecurities we must face

Were imperfect, flawed, but that's okay

As long as we strive to be better every day

We must acknowledge our dark side exists

And work to control it, so it doesn't persist

For only then can we truly be free

Of the darkness that threatens our humanity.

Define

In a room filled with people,

I feel this void, blank expression,

Just like a dry leaf of maple,

As it falls, yet filled with composition,

Even if I'm a pawn on the chess board,

The main death in my hands may,

Not every spirit is killed by a sword,

Blood covered in mud as I lay,

A hollow lingering on me divine,

An unsolved mystery mastermind,

But will you compare ham to swine,

Even chains can't bear to bind,

A touch of death on my fingertips,

I may physically seem still,

Poisoned may be your dips,

I can change your mind on my will,

I stand at the edge of the bridge,

And words flow like a river,

Not all battles start with a ridge,

Won't let you drown in ice,

But will make sure you shiver.

Night

The vibrant orange sets the day,

Its tint slowly fading away,

The shadows advance, leading in,

It's a silent fierce win,

Glitter scattered across the sky,

Mesmerized not ready to die,

One of them is named after me,

For every deed you're charged a fee,

Like a stolen jewel from Caesar's crown,

Proceeding like brute, in statement don't drown,

I come before time, to you warn,

You've been with strategies born,

Engulfed by a hole, black and old,

The night begins with a spark bold.

From The Dead Poets Society

Oh captain, my captain,

Lead us to the land of truth,

Where poetry reigns supreme,

And the values of life bear fruit,

For in the hallowed halls of Welton,

The Dead Poets Society thrives,

A brotherhood of free thinkers,

With passions that never subside,

They value creativity and expression,

In a world that demands conformity,

They believe in seizing the day,

And pursuing one's own destiny,

The poetry of life is their guide,

As they seek to make a difference,

To inspire, to challenge, to dream,

And to break away from indifference,

Their spirits soar with every verse,

As they embrace the beauty of words,

And find meaning in every moment,

No matter how fleeting or absurd,

 So let us all heed their call,

To live boldly, to love fiercely,

And to embrace the values of The Dead Poets Society,

For they offer us a way to truly be free,

Oh captain, my captain,

We shall follow your lead,

And honor the legacy of the poets,

Whose values we shall forever heed.

Underwater

Beneath the waves, I find myself,

Submerged in the depths, without a sound or help,

The world above fades away, as I sink down,

Embraced by the silence, no light, no sound,

The pressure builds, squeezing my chest,

As I struggle for breath, with no relief or rest,

The darkness engulfs me, as I sink deeper still,

With no way out, no hope, no will,

Yet in the silence, I find a strange peace,

As I ease towards the end, my struggles cease,

The water surrounds me, calming my fears,

And I let go of my worries, my doubts, my tears,

The world above seems far away,

As I sink further, towards the light of day,

The silence envelops me, like a warm embrace,

As I surrender to the deep, with no trace,

The end draws near, but I feel no fear,

As I embrace the silence, and draw near,

For in this moment, I find a strange solace,

In the depths of the water, with no malice,

And as I sink down, towards the unknown,

I find a peace, a calmness, a new home,

For in the silence, I find a strange beauty,

As I let go, and embrace the end, with no duty.

Volume 1

As I read these words upon the page,

I feel a stirring deep within,

My heart beats faster, like a sage,

Whose wisdom flows from deep within,

Each phrase and verse is like a spell,

That casts a spell upon my soul,

And as I read, I feel compelled,

To let these feelings take control,

The words themselves seem to come alive,

A dance of rhythm, rhyme, and sound,

As if they strive to strive and strive,

To make their meaning all around,

And as I read, I feel them stir,

A surge of passion, joy, and pain,

Each line a gem, a precious blur,

That I must grasp, and hold, and gain,

For words are more than mere ideas,

They're feelings, thoughts, and dreams made real,

A language that can move and please,

And touch the heart with lasting zeal,

So let me read and feel these words,

Let them flow through me and ignite,

A fire that burns, and stirs, and urges,

And fills my soul with pure delight.

I Am

I am a canvas, woven with threads of hues

The elements of qualities, like a prism's views

A riddle to decipher, a puzzle to unfold

A cloth of contradictions, ever- changing and bold

My words flow like a river, with the force of a storm

My moves glide like a swan, with grace that transforms

My voice echoes like thunder, with a melody that sings

My strokes paint like magic, with colors that bring

My dreams soar like an eagle, to the heavens above

My actions charge like a lion, with strength and love

My stories unravel like a tapestry, of times gone by

My tales untold like a mystery, waiting to defy

I am unique, a rare gem in a world of clones

My personality and talents, a bouquet of unknowns

No comparison to make, for I am like none

The sum of all I am, a fusion that shines like the sun.

He Is A Boy

A boy is told to be strong and bold
To never show his tears or fold
For he must be the rock that holds
His family, wife, and friends in their roles

He's taught to be the provider and the hero
To protect and defend, and never let go
To put his own needs and fears aside
And be the man that he must abide

For his mom, he must be the support
The one she can count on for comfort
For his wife, he must be the pillar
The one who holds her close, never to wither

For his daughter, he must be the guide
The one who teaches her to thrive
To be strong, kind, and wise
And never let anyone dim her light

For his friends, he must be the leader

The one who inspires and helps them discover

Their own strength and potential

And to never give up, always be resolute

And for himself, he must find a way

To balance it all, to never sway

To be true to his heart and soul

And never let the pressure take its toll

So a boy becomes a man, through the years

Learning to face his doubts and fears

But always remembering the roles he must play

To be strong and not cry, come what may.

She Is A Girl

A girl child born into the world
With a future so bright and bold
But as she grows, she learns the truth
The world is harsh and often crude

Her burden starts when she's young
Expected to be seen, not heard nor fun
Taught to be gentle, meek and mild
And never to question or get wild

As she grows into a woman
Her burden weighs heavily on her shoulders
Expected to balance work and home
And to never let either one falter

She's judged by her beauty, not her mind
And her worth is often left behind
Expected to fit into a mold
Of what society wants her to behold

The pressure to be perfect is high
And every flaw is magnified
Her body is objectified and owned
And her dreams are often postponed

But she is strong, and she will rise
Above the burden that lies
She'll break free from society's mold
And embrace her own path, bold and gold

She'll fight for her rights, and for others too
And prove that a girl child can do
Anything she sets her mind to
And in the end, she'll make it through.

Convo

She sat pondering the meaning of life,

A weight on her shoulders, a sense of strife,

An adult sat beside her with a wise old face,

And at that moment, a conversation took place.

She asked, "What is the meaning of life?

What really matters in this world of strife?"

The adult replied with a kind-hearted tone,

"Love is what matters, it makes a heart feel at home."

"But what about success and material gain?"

She asked with a hint of disdain,

"Those things are nice, but they do not define,

The true value of life, the treasures we find."

The teen was confused, for she had been told,

That success and wealth were worth more than gold,

But the adult explained, with a gentle voice,

"That love and kindness are a much greater choice."

She then asked, with a sense of despair,

"How do we survive, when the world is unfair?"

The adult smiled and said, "It's not easy to do,

But we must persevere, and see it through."

For life is a journey, with ups and downs,

And sometimes were lost, sometimes were found,

But if we hold on to love, and do what is right,

We'll find our way, in the darkest of night.

What Is Frustration?

Frustration, oh how it feels so bleak,

Leaving us powerless, helpless, and weak,

Like waTer trapped in a maze we cannot escape,

Feeling like we're caught in a never- ending scrape.

But is frustration always such a bad thing?

Can it push us forward and help us to sing?

Or is it merely a stepping stone,

To a deeper anger, that is often shown?

Anger, a natural emotion, they say,

But when does it lead us astray?

When we let it consume us whole,

And it takes over our mind and soul.

But can we really control our rage,

When it feels like we're locked in a cage?

Is it worth the effort to hold it in,

Or should we just let the fury begin?

Perhaps it's all about balance and control,

Learning to manage our emotions as a whole,

For giving in to anger may feel good in the moment,

But it can lead to regret and torment.

So let us question our frustration and rage,

And find ways to manage and engage,

For in doing so, we may find a happier life,

And peace within the chaos and strife.

Time's A Maze

Within the belly of the beast,
Cold steel glows with apathy unleashed
No need for hands to operate
Serviced by motors monstrous in weight

Its self-sufficiency a grim sight
It never yields our just plight
Maze-like, with no switch to end
Its ceaseless hissing, whirring, a monotonous blend

All invited, to the back or front
Their minds numb, blissful, to be blunt
All come for its services to claim
By the brute's majesty, a lure to fame

A pilgrimage preordained, not by choice
Its structure, unworldly, cold, and devoid of voice
Standing tall on pillars icy and bare
Nothing warm in its existence, a truth hard to bear

As my tour continues, office doors shut

Behind them, judges, who determine our but

But who are they to judge and discern

With variables and virtues too many to learn

Unable to fathom its inner working

The chamber that most regard with reverence lurking

And some with a terror of two lifetimes

Like others, I too will face its shadows, the next lemming
in line

Succeeding the ones before, preceding those yet to pass

Within the belly of the beast, a fate we cannot surpass

For the machine grinds on, relentless in its grind

A reminder of our insignificance, in the grand scheme of
mankind.

Nightmare

In slumber's grasp, I'm ensnared

By nightmares fierce and unprepared

Their grip on me, a clasp so tight

I struggle and writhe in the grip of the night

Like a storm, they rage and howl

A tempest of fear that makes me scowl

I try to escape, to flee the fray

But I'm trapped in this dark and dismal play

My mind's eye sees a world undone

A desolate wasteland, devoid of sun

My soul, like a bird with clipped wings

Falls from the sky and shatters into a million

I question everyone for your location

But nobody knows, it's a hallucination

I'm trapped in this horror, can't break free

Screaming for help, but no one can hear me

Rustic neighbors offer their hospitality

But it's a trap, a banquet of brutality

The guests on the table, drinking a disgusting brew

My plate enabled with human flesh stew

I scream to the stars, covered in gashes

This world is upside down, full of ashes

But there's no trace of you, it's a nightmare

A terror so deep, I can't even share

I try to wake up, to escape this hell

But itTs like I'm under a cursed spell.

I pray for dawn to break this night

And save me from this endless fright.

Unreal

Ditch my fake buddies,

Now I am unsteady,

I was always there for them,

I want to to over-live this gen,

Like the rain I keep falling,

I might even wait for the calling,

You show yourself the victim,

And make me love the villain,

Reality is despising,

Is god gonna help me, reviving?

Favoritism ,why does it exist?

Idealism is what I insist?

Unreal are the words they speak,

But I know without me they are weak,

Slagging is what they do,

They don't show what is true,

Known for one bright side,

Can't they see the shadow beside,

There is something wrong with this lost connections,

We live in one world but different dimensions,

So I choose to remain cryptic,

To see the real me ,you need more than an optic.

Society

Society, a merciless beast,

Devouring us all with its feast,

Driving us all to the brink,

A gun to my head, I can't even think.

The bullet's sound echoes loud,

As I fall to the ground,

Blood flowing like a river,

But just a few drops, don't quiver.

I'm just a maniac, insane,

With no remorse or pain,

But then I see her tears,

Real and full of fears.

No funeral for me,

Just flames to set me free,

But she fights with all her might,

And I'm so proud of her, it's a painful sight.

My soul is pulled back to life,

A second chance to survive,

Choking and bewildered faces,

Am I meant to die in two places?

The grenade falls, a symbol of our fight,

As we watch them burn, it feels so right,

The oppressors suffer, as they should,

Our smile of relief, pure and good.

Society, a murderer with no remorse,

But we'll fight back with all our force,

And when we finally win this war,

We'll go back to where we belong, forevermore.

Purpose

We often ask, why are we here?

What's life's purpose, far and near?

Is it a game of cosmic chance,

Or something more, beyond our glance?

We scour books and faith for clues,

And seek meaning in the things we choose,

But the question haunts us all the same,

WhatTs the reason for life's game?

Is it to chase after bliss,

Or to leave a mark that we'll miss?

Is it to better the world we see,

Or to simply exist and be free?

As we ponder, the mysteries unfold,

And we realize, in a way untold,

That lifeTs purpose may be just to live,

To take chances and to give.

To learn and love, to grow and change,

And to face every joy and pain,

To chart our own path in this world,

And create a legacy that unfurls.

So let us savor every moment,

And live with purpose and intent,

For through life's journey may be brief,

Our impact can bring eternal relief.

Chilly Aura

Arctic ashes, cold and bright,

Illuminate the darkest night,

But what do they reveal?

What does reality conceal?

Behind the curtains, lies a world,

 Of secrets, lies, and stories unfurled,

A game of pretend, we all must play,

To get through each and every day.

Crystal flames a spark of light,

Reveal the truth, but only in sight,

For the reality we see,

Is not always what it seems to be.

We hide behind masks, we wear a disguise,

Pretending to be someone else, telling lies,

But deep down, we all feel the cold,

The icy truth, we can't withhold.

Winter blazes, a glimmer of hope,

A light in the darkness, a way to cope,

With the reality we face each day,

And the masks we wear, come what may.

So let the cold spark illuminate,

The truth we hide, the lies we state,

For in the end, it's only the truth,

That can set us free from the pretend game's booth.

Aamina Sadiya Ali

Beyond
The Surface

Desire

Life without desire can be dull and gray,

Stagnant and unfulfilling every day,

Desires give us motivation to strive,

Set goals and work hard to stay alive.

Big or small, it doesn't matter,

Desires give us purpose and chatter,

To strive for something better every day,

And find direction in life in every way.

Desires help us grow and take flight,

Contribute to society with our might,

When we have a desire we take action,

And make a positive impact without distraction.

But it's important to find balance within,

Desires that align with our values to win,

True fulfillment comes from deep inside,

And finding happiness in desires we can't hide.

So don't be afraid to set your sights high,

And chase after your desires until you touch the sky,

In conclusion, desires are what we need,

To live a fulfilling life with purpose and speed.

Inner Critic

Your inner critic, always lurking deep,

Inside our minds, where it loves to creep,

It tells us lies, it feeds us doubt,

It keeps us small, it holds us down,

It tells us we're not good enough,

That we'll never measure up,

It tells us we're too fat or thin,

Too bright or dumb, too weak to even begin,

But your inner critic is just a voice,

It's not the truth, it's just a choice,

We have the power to silence it,

To rise above and not submit,

So let's stand tall and embrace our worth,

Let's shout out loud and let it burst,

We are amazing, we are unique,

We have the power, we cannot be beat,

So let's ignore the inner critic's lies,

And embrace our strength, our beauty, our lives,

For we are capable, we are worthy,

We must delete the blur and stand firmly.

Hypergraphia

Writing random words here and there,

Isn't it just a creative despair,

There's a problem in my brain they say,

Am I not really okay?

Pushing the strokes through the pages,

Drawing a pile of sawdust and ashes,

Noting down my thoughts or making a random list,

Why is it so difficult for me to exist?

Sometimes it's stars and sometimes its others,

Once was a sky filled with wonders,

It isn't distressing I guarantee,

Is there something wrong with me?

Scribbling too much or leaving less space,

All I can do is embrace,

My Mind always wanting to detail,

Are u hoping its a fairytale?

Fashionista

Find your fashion flow, let it take you high,

Express yourself in style, let your colors fly,

Play with patterns, mix and match with glee,

Personal style is all about being you, you see!

Join the fashion revolution, let your true self show,

Rock your look with confidence, let your style glow,

Make a statement with your wardrobe,
stand out from the crowd,

Find your fashion flow, let your style be proud!

Confidence is key, when it comes to fashion,

It's not about following, it's about expression,

Step outside your comfort zone, try something new,

You'll find what makes you feel confident and true!

From runway shows to street style,
fashion is everywhere,

A way to connect with others, a form of self-care,

So go ahead and join the fun, let your style come alive,

Find your fashion flow, let it thrive!

Your clothes are your canvas, your style is your art,

So embrace it, own it, be confident and smart!

Find your fashion flow and let your style shine,

In this fashion revolution, you'll always be divine!

The Fate Of Doubt

Self-doubt, a dark cloud that lingers

A weight that makes the heart feel heavier

A bird with wings, but still, it fears

The wind's whispers, a voice that jeers

The desk, a place of work and strife

Where the crowd tells her to shine bright

But one wrong move, and she's cast aside

Judged, criticized, left with wounded pride

A flower, with seeds planted deep

Expected to bloom, to fragrance keep

But withered, it's left alone to weep

For not living up to the expectations steep

She cries and sighs, alone in her bed

Wondering if she'll ever get ahead

Self-doubt a thought that fills her head

"Is this fate?" a question left unsaid

But with every doubt and fear that's felt

A glimmer of hope within her dwells

For though the winds may howl and pelt

The bird still flies, and the flower still swells.

Confidunt Exitibus

Verifying trust is a must,

Else it will turn to rust,

In relationships, it's a must,

Else it will turn to dust,

To trust someone blindly,

Is not wise, you see,

It's better to verify,

And then trust carefully,

Trust should be earned,

Not just given,

To make sure it's not spurned,

Verification is needed to be driven,

Trust should be nurtured,

Not taken for granted,

It should be cherished,

And not be slanted,

Verifying trust is essential,

To make sure it's not accidental,

It's not a one-time thing,

But a continuous process that needs to ring,

Verifying trust is a must,

Else it will turn to rust,

It's not something to be taken lightly,

Else it will turn out to be quite flighty.

Small Acts, Big Impact

Through chilly streets I walked alone

With thoughts consumed by harshness shown

News filled with hate and violence

Injustice rampant, no silence

But then, a spark caught my eye

A glimmering light, so bright it shined

At first I thought, just a reflection

But as I drew near, my heart's affection

I felt awe wash over me

As I watched them with humility

People who had every reason to be bitter

Choosing instead to spread love and glitter

In that moment, I saw with clarity

Sparks of goodness in the world with rarity

Even in the coldest of times

Warmth and kindness still shine

As I walked on, I noticed more

Small acts of warmth, goodness and rapport

A stranger helping the elderly cross the street

A child sharing toys with someone to meet

These small acts, so powerful and true

Reminded me of the good we can do

No matter how cold and dark it may seem

There's always light, a spark to redeem

Amidst freezing coldness,

The spirt of happiness,

Though I can't change everything, it's clear

A spark of goodness can inspire, draw near.

Fan Girl

She stands in the crowd, her heart beating fast

As the music starts and the stage is cast

The boy band comes on, and she feels the thrill

Of the lyrics that speak to her heart and will

She's a fangirl, through and through

One Direction is her favorite crew

Their music fills her soul with glee

And their lyrics speak to her endlessly

She talks to them as if they're real

In her mind, they're more than a deal

Their words give her hope, and she dreams

Of a life where they're the only team

But alas, she's just one in the crowd

No one notices her, no one's allowed

To know that her love for them runs deep

And she longs for them to take the leap

To see her and know that she's there

That their words are more than just air

That they touch her heart and soul

And make her feel like she's whole

But until that day comes, she'll stand and sway

To the beat of the music that they play

And dream of the conversations they'd have

If only they knew how much she was their fan.

Aamina Sadiya Ali

States Of Mind

Just Some Fears

The fear of opinion, a heavy chain,

That keeps us bound and feeling restrained,

We fear the judgment of those around,

And keep our true selves tightly wound.

The fear of being alone, a haunting thought,

That keeps us seeking company sought,

We fear the silence and its toll,

And dread the void that takes its hold.

The fear of imperfection, a constant weight,

That makes us fear our every mistake,

We fear the flaw that we possess,

And fear the world's harsh, critical press.

The fear of being afraid, a paradoxical fear,

That keeps us frozen and unable to steer,

We fear the fear that grips our heart,

And fear the paralysis that sets us apart.

The fear of weakness, a hidden foe,

That makes us fear to let our feelings show,

We fear the vulnerability we feel,

And fear the judgment that others deal.

The fear of emotional and physical pain,

A fear that seems to drive us insane,

We fear the hurt that life can bring,

And fear the toll that pain can ring.

The fear of unknown, a dread profound,

That keeps us rooted to the ground,

We fear the future that lies ahead,

And fear the path that we must tread.

The fear of losing someone we love,

A fear that grips us like a glove,

We fear the void that death can bring,

And fear the grief that we must sing.

From Dreams
To Reality

She's lost in her thoughts,

Reading, writing, poetry sought,

But something strange began to brew,

As she saw things not in view,

At first just flickers in her eye,

Then a woman, smile so spry,

Appeared at random times each day,

And she felt like they were okay,

But a world, so magical and grand,

Soon came into view, at her command,

Hours lost exploring, making friends,

Her imagination knew no ends,

Things from this world she'd bring back,

A new parchment or a pen with an unusual rock,

Her poetry captured the beauty she had seen,

In this other world, so serene,

But a realization struck so deep,

That this world, just in her sleep,

Was simply a work of her mind,

The pain of letting go, so unkind,

Her words then changed, no longer the same,

Writing of beauty in the real world's frame,

For she found that magic exists here too,

In the real world, just like in her view,

She cherished the memories, lessons learned,

But it was time to focus, time to discern,

The wonders the real world could offer,

With her imagination, she'd never suffer.

Spirit Of Writing

The spirit of writing is elusive,

A muse that comes and goes,

Sometimes a gentle breeze,

Other times a fierce wind that blows,

It whispers secrets in your ear,

And fills your mind with ideas,

It inspires you to create,

And helps you conquer your fears,

It gives voice to the voiceless,

And brings forth tales untold,

It captures moments in time,

And turns them into gold,

The spirit of writing is a flame,

That burns bright in your soul,

It fuels your passion and drive,

And makes you feel whole,

So let your pen flow freely,

And let your words take flight,

For the spirit of writing is with you,

Guiding you through the night.

We Think

We are masters of overthinking,
Fuelled by fear and doubt,
Our minds play out every scenario,
Every "what if" is given clout.

We suffer in our thoughts,
As if they were reality,
Spending tears on an unpredictable future,
One that may never come to be.

We grip onto our worries,
Like a vice that won't let go,
As if we can control the outcome,
But really, we just suffer in our own echo.

Our minds become a battleground,
As we fight against ourselves,
Our fears and doubts like weapons,
That harm us more than any external cells.

We create a storm of chaos,
In a world that's yet to unfold,
We torture ourselves with the possibilities,
And forget that life is meant to be bold.

We must learn to release our grip,
On the things we cannot control,
To live in the present moment,
And let the future unfold.

For in the end, the future is unpredictable,
And we can't control what will come to pass,
So let's not spend our tears on what could be,
And instead, live our lives with a little more sass.

Let's be brave in the face of uncertainty,
And embrace the unknown,
For it's in these moments of discomfort,
That we truly grow and are shown.

So let go of your worries and fears,
And live your life with zeal,
For the future is just a concept,
And the present is where the magic is real.

Do You Believe In Magic? Why Not?

The term "magic" does not
 always imply something supernatural,

If you ask how? here is your answer-

Do you think books can not take you to a different place
you never imagined going to?

Do you think magic is what magicians do?

Do you think creations by humans are not magic?

Do you think magic is something that has to have logic?

Do you think of magic as non existing?

Do you think there is no magic
when there is an unusual sighting?

Well if you think of these above and more,
I am here to push you through a door,

Now look on your left and you will see,
an enchanted place full of mystery,

Turn to your right and enjoy the view,
of a breathtaking space hue,

Focus out front and walk toward,
the fascinating rare bird,

Look up and cherish the sight,
of grass growing way up in the sky,

Just peek a bit below you, if you're scared of horror too,

Blink for a moment and see, your surroundings
change pretty quickly,

Now take a minute a check if you could imagine
even one from the above,

If you could, do you not see,
how I answered your first question,

Was this not magic? if you still do not believe,
 I would like to answer the next,

Magicians use illusions,
they show you their different tricks,

They craft a special performance when repeated fades,

He will make you believe an illusion,
only a few can look past,

If you are among the many, I would still want to
convince you,

Magic has no logic, it can make
you take you inside a comic,

Magic is not trickery, but it is surely satisfactory,

Magic does not burst out of a wand, it is just
superabound.

Past, Huh?

The past is a mysterious place,

Full of stories, memories, and faces,

Sometimes we long to go back,

To a time that we once knew, and we lack,

But is the past worth revisiting?

Or is it time to move on and keep living?

It's a question that's hard to answer,

But perhaps it's worth considering,

The past can hold important lessons,

That can shape the present and future sessions,

But it can also be a burden,

If we let it weigh us down and hinder,

So perhaps the best course of action,

Is to find a balance, a healthy fraction,

We can learn from the past, but not be held back,

We can move on, but not forget the track,

The past is worth revisiting, to a degree,

But it's also important to set it free,

So we can live in the present, and look ahead,

To a bright future, with no regrets or dread.

Eating Disorder

Eating disorders, a foe so cruel,

A challenge that many teens do duel,

When stress comes knocking at the door,

They start to feel they can't take it anymore.

Anorexia, where food becomes the enemy,

A trap that's hard to break free,

Restricting food, a sense of control,

But the damage to the body takes its toll.

Bulimia, where purging is the key,

A cycle that's hard to break free,

Eating too much, feeling the guilt,

Vomiting after, feeling like their life is wilt.

Binge-eating disorder, where food is a refuge,

A way to escape, a temporary truce,

Eating without control, feeling the shame,

A never-ending cycle that seems to have no aim.

These disorders are a burden to bear,
A challenge that many teens do share,
But there's hope, there's light,
There's a way to make things right.

Seeking help is the first step,
A way to overcome this depth,
Talking to someone who understands,
A way to get back on solid land.

It's not a battle that can be fought alone,
Support and care are the cornerstone,
A journey of healing, step by step,
A way to break free from this trap.

Eating disorders may seem like a wall,
But with help, it's not impossible to stand tall
A brighter future lies ahead,
Where positivity and hope spread.

Best Friends

Eleven years of laughter and tears,

Of shared secrets and endless cheers,

Of growing up and growing together,

Of being each other's shelter.

Two best friends, just two girls,

Their bond unbreakable, like precious pearls,

Through thick and thin, they stood by each other,

And nothing could ever smother.

They met as young girls, with so much to learn,

And now, they've blossomed into beautiful women,

But their friendship is still as strong as ever,

A true testament to a bond that will never sever.

They've faced challenges, and overcome them all,

With each other's support, they'll never fall,

They know each other's strengths and flaws,

And they love each other, despite it all.

Eleven years may seem like a long time,

But for these two, it feels like just a dime,

Their friendship has grown and matured,

And their bond will forever endure.

So here's to these two best friends,

May their friendship never end,

May they continue to grow and thrive,

And cherish each other for all their lives.

I Hate

I hate the sun that shines so bright,

Makes the days so long I have to work and strive,

I hate the stars that twinkle at night,

Misleading the way to the campsite.

I hate the birds that chirp and sing,

Causing noise ,making my ears ring,

I hate the joy that life can bring,

As it takes it just as quickly in a blink.

I hate the flowers that bloom in May,

And by the next month just wither away,

I hate the children that laugh and play,

Cause I wasn't constrained to stay.

I hate the warmth that's in the air,

Lying about what we care,

I hate the happy faces that's everywhere,

Faking a smile regardless of despair.

I hate the friends that come and go,
After giggles ,tears come by ,that's what they do,
I hate the memories that I know,
Filled with pain and pressure so.

I hate the dreams that never came true,
Making me feel ill never get through,
I hate the fact that I'm feeling blue,
The shaken frame in my view.

I hate the world that's full of pain,
The failure inspire of strain,
I hate the hope that's all in vain,
Both ambition and expectations slain.

I hate the faith that's hard to find,
It slips and slides in my mind,
I hate the truth that's so unkind,
As you can now see thing to which you were blind.

I hate the life that lacked vision,
Cause I'm always falling just to be risen,
I hate the reason that I'm livin',
Cause everything is decided by my virtue and sin.

I hate everything that's in my sight,

Cause I am living without the right

I hate it all with all my might,

Anyways I have to be my own knight.

I Love

I love the books that take me away,

To lands of wonder and mystery,

Where I can lose myself for hours on end,

And forget all my misery.

My poetry, my heart and soul,

My words that flow like a river,

Expressing my deepest thoughts and feelings,

Bringing me joy that will never wither.

My family, my pillars of strength,

Who stand by me through thick and thin,

Their love and support, an unbreakable bond,

A treasure that keeps me from caving in.

My friends, my companions on this journey,

Who laugh with me and dry my tears,

Their presence a aura to my weary soul,

A comfort that eases my fears.

My skills, my talents that make me unique,

That bring me pride and a sense of worth,

A reminder that I have something to offer,

A reason to strive and prove my birth.

The moon, a celestial beauty above,

Its tranquil light, like a charming swan,

A gentle reminder of the vastness of life,

And the peace that can be found in calm.

Coffee, the aroma that lifts my spirits,

Its rich flavour, a warmth in my soul,

A simple pleasure that brings me joy,

And helps me face life's challenges as a whole.

The smell of earth after rain, a fresh scent,

That awakens my senses and fills me with glee,

A reminder of life's renewal and growth,

And the hope that the future will be.

Music, the rhythm that moves my soul,

Its melody, a language that speaks to my heart,

A timeless gift that transcends all boundaries,

And unites us all, from end to start.

The ripples of water, a gentle dance,

That soothes my spirit and calms my mind,

A reminder of the ebb and flow of life,

And the resilience that we can always find.

The black sky, a canvas of endless possibility,

Its vastness, a reminder of the unknown,

A mystery waiting to be discovered,

And an adventure waiting to be shown.

And lastly, me, a flawed and beautiful being,

With dreams and fears, hopes and doubts,

But with a spirit that never gives up,

And the courage to face life's constant bouts.